CRAFTSMEN,
TRADERS, AND
FEARSOME RAIDERS

THE REAL
VIKINGS

MELVIN BERGER AND
GILDA BERGER

NATIONAL GEOGRAPHIC

WASHINGTON, D.C.

For Dagmar, with love
—M.B. and G.B.

Many thanks to Richard N. Ringler, former professor of English and Scandinavian studies at the University of Wisconsin-Madison, for his expert review of the text and pictures.

Copyright © 2003 Melvin Berger

Published by the National Geographic Society. All rights reserved. Reproduction of the whole or any part of the contents without written permission from the National Geographic Society is strictly prohibited.

Published by the National Geographic Society
John M. Fahey, Jr., President and Chief Executive Officer
Gilbert M. Grosvenor, Chairman of the Board
Nina D. Hoffman, Executive Vice President,
        President of Books and Education Publishing Group
Ericka Markman, Senior Vice President,
        President, Children's Books and Education Publishing Group

Staff for this book:
Nancy Laties Feresten, Vice President,
        Editor-in-Chief, Children's Books
Bea Jackson, Art Director, Children's Books
Jo Tunstall, Project Editor
Bea Jackson and Dan Sherman, Designers
Alison Eskildsen, Illustrations Editor
Janet Dustin, Illustrations Coordinator
Marfé Ferguson Delano, Editor
Carl Mehler, Director of Maps
Nicholas P. Rosenbach, Map Research
Gregory Ugiansky, Map Production
Martin S. Walz, Map Production
Julia Marshall, Indexer
R. Gary Colbert, Production Director
Lewis R. Bassford, Production Manager
Vincent P. Ryan, Manufacturing Manager

Front Cover: Viking raiders prepare to invade France in this illustration from a ninth-century manuscript.
Back Cover: This carved wooden figurehead of a dragon once graced the bow of an early Viking ship.
Half-Title Page: A picture carved on a shaped piece of limestone shows a ship filled with dead Viking warriors on their way to Valhalla, the Viking heaven.
Title Page: Sixteenth-century manuscript of *Egil's Saga*, which was first written in 13th-century Iceland.

Library of Congress Cataloging-in-Publication Data
Berger, Melvin.
The Real Vikings: Craftsmen, Traders, and Fearsome Raiders / Melvin and Gilda Berger.
p. cm.
ISBN 0-7922-5132-6 (hardcover)
1. Vikings. 2. Civilization, Viking. 3. Northmen. I. Berger, Gilda.
II. Title.
DL65.B45 2003   948'.022—dc21   2002154474

Printed in Belgium

Illustrations Credits
Cover, Bibliotheque Nationale, Paris; Back cover, C.M. Dixon; Case cover, Courtesy National Museum of Iceland; Half-title page, Archivo Iconografico, S.A./CORBIS; Title page, Jóhanna Ólafsdottir, Arni Magnusson Institute; Contents page, Jóhanna Ólafsdottir, Arni Magnusson Institute; 2, Ted Spiegel; 4, Sisse Brimberg; 5 (upper), Ted Spiegel/CORBIS; 5 (lower), Ted Spiegel/CORBIS; 6 (upper), Bengt A. Lundberg/Riksantikvarieambetet; 6 (lower), from "The Viking World," Frances Lincoln Publishers Limited; 7, Courtesy Stofnun Arna Maenussonar; 8, Ted Spiegel/CORBIS; 10 (upper left), Louis S. Glanzman; 10 (upper right), Courtesy Penguin Books Limited; 10 (lower left), Courtesy Peter Harholdt, Smithsonian Institution, NMNH; 10 (lower right), Courtesy Peter Harholdt, Smithsonian Institution, NMNH; 11, Statens Historiska Museum; 12 (upper), Courtesy Penguin Books Limited; 12 (lower left), Courtesy The County Museum of Gotland; 12 (lower right), Courtesy Smithsonian Institution, NMNH; 14 (upper) Statens Historiska Museum; 14 (lower left), Richard T. Nowitz; 14 (lower right), Courtesy Smithsonian Institution, NMNH; 15, C.M. Dixon; 16, Courtesy Stofnun Arna Maenussonar; 18 (left), Courtesy Smithsonian Institution, NMNH; 18 (right), Sisse Brimberg; 19 (upper left), Ted Spiegel; 19 (right), Courtesy Stofnun Arna Maenussonar; 19 (lower left), Statens Historiska Museum; 20 (upper), Richard T. Nowitz; 20 (lower), Courtesy National Museum of Scotland; 21 (upper), Courtesy Stofnun Arna Maenussonar; 21 (lower), Werner Forman/Art Resource, NY; 22, Tim Thompson/CORBIS; 23, Louis S. Glanzman; 24, Louis S. Glanzman; 26, Courtesy The University of Oslo; 27 (upper), Barbara L. Gibson; 27 (lower left), Richard T. Nowitz; 27 (lower right), Werner Forman Archive/Art Resource, NY; 28 (upper), Courtesy The University of Oslo; 28 (lower), Statens Historiska Museum; 29, Louis S. Glanzman; 30, Courtesy Stofnun Arna Maenussonar; 31, Richard T. Nowitz; 32, Art Resource, NY; 35, Louis S. Glanzman; 36, Courtesy Stofnun Arna Maenussonar; 38 (left), Werner Forman/Art Resource, NY; 38 (right), Statens Historiska Museum; 39, Bettmann/Corbis; 40, Mary Evans Picture Library, London; 42 (upper), Bjorn Backe/Papilio/Corbis; 42 (lower), Courtesy Stofnun Arna Maenussonar; 43, Sisse Brimberg; 44, Louis S. Glanzman; 45, Courtesy Stofnun Arna Maenussonar; 47, Macduff Everton/CORBIS; 48, Courtesy The University of Oslo; 49, Courtesy Stofnun Arna Maenussonar; 50, Strauss/Curtis/Corbis; 52 (upper), Craig Lassig/Corbis; 52 (lower), Courtesy Peter Harholdt, Smithsonian Institution, NMNH; 53, Ted Spiegel/Corbis; 54, Christe Åhlin, The Museum of National Antiquities, Sweden.

CONTENTS

Boldly drawn illustrations adorn a page from the *Reykjabok,* an Icelandic law code regarding shipping on the high seas.

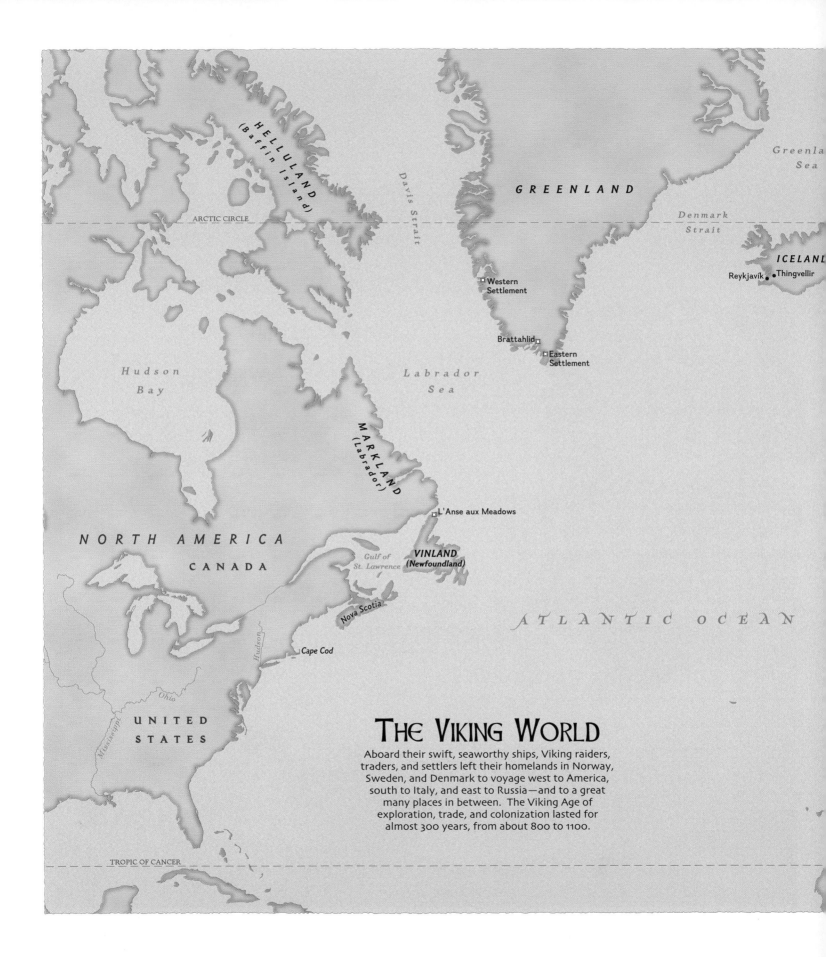

HELLULAND
(Baffin Island)

Davis Strait

GREENLAND

*Greenla
Sea*

ARCTIC CIRCLE

*Denmark
Strait*

ICELAN

Reykjavík • Thingvellir

□ Western
Settlement

*Hudson
Bay*

*Labrador
Sea*

Brattahlid □

□ Eastern
Settlement

MARKLAND
(Labrador)

□ L'Anse aux Meadows

NORTH AMERICA

CANADA

*Gulf of
St. Lawrence*

VINLAND
(Newfoundland)

Nova Scotia

Hudson

ATLANTIC OCEAN

Cape Cod

Ohio

UNITED
STATES

Mississippi

THE VIKING WORLD

Aboard their swift, seaworthy ships, Viking raiders,
traders, and settlers left their homelands in Norway,
Sweden, and Denmark to voyage west to America,
south to Italy, and east to Russia—and to a great
many places in between. The Viking Age of
exploration, trade, and colonization lasted for
almost 300 years, from about 800 to 1100.

TROPIC OF CANCER

ARCTIC OCEAN

Norwegian Sea

ARCTIC CIRCLE

FINLAND

Faroe Islands

NORWAY

Lake Ladoga

● Bergen

Oseberg ● ● Oslo SWEDEN

Shetland
Islands

● Staraya Ladoga

Volkhov R.

Gokstad ●

● Birka

Novgorod ●

● Orkney Islands

rides

SCANDINAVIA

RUSSIA

ASIA

SCOTLAND

North Sea

● Riga

† Lindisfarne

Vorbasse ● ● Jelling

DENMARK

Baltic Sea

W. Dvina

● York

Hedeby ●

Volga

Bulgar ●

● Dublin ENGLAND

IRELAND

WALES

NETH.

GERMANY

Elbe

Oder

Vistula

Kiev ●

London ●
Hastings ✕

Prague ●

Dnieper

Volga

Volgograd ●

UKRAINE

Don

English Channel

Normandy ● Paris

EUROPE

Seine

(Astrakhan) Itil ●

Rhine

*Aral
Sea*

Loire

FRANCE

Danube

Black Sea

Caspian Sea

Amu Darya

Chorezm ●

Bay of
Biscay

Rhône

Luna ●

ITALY

Mediterranean

Rome ●

Constantinople ●
(Istanbul)

Baku ●

Bukhara ● ● Samarqand

PORTUGAL

SPAIN

GREECE

TURKEY

Strait of Gibraltar

Tigris

Gorgan ●

Sea

Euphrates

Alexandria ●

● Jerusalem

Baghdad ●

PERSIA
(IRAN)

EGYPT

Nile

Red Sea

Persian Gulf

AFRICA

TROPIC OF CANCER

● Town
□ Settlement
† Monastery
✕ Battle site

0 _____ 500 mi
0 _____ 800 km

CHAPTER ONE

WHO WERE THE VIKINGS?

t is June 8 in A.D. 793. Light is dawning on the tiny island of Lindisfarne, off the northeast coast of England. The monks of the island's monastery awaken to the clangor of the chapel's bells. Some peek out to look at the sea from behind the thick monastery walls. They watch carefully as a cluster of black-hulled ships slowly advances toward shore.

As the ships draw closer, the monks see perhaps a hundred men in each ship. Some of the men are pulling hard on long, heavy oars. Standing tall between the seated rowers are husky warriors, some with their faces hidden behind tight, shiny helmets. One after another, the ships noisily scrape onto the rocky beach. The fighters tumble over the sides of the ships and rush forward, wildly swinging their swords and battle-axes above their heads. With loud whoops and hollers, the invaders storm into the monastery and fall upon the frightened monks.

Some monks flee and hide. Others dash into the church. The frenzied Viking attackers catch many of the religious men—and slaughter them. The rest the Vikings drive to their deaths in the sea or bind up to be taken away as slaves.

Not yet done, the raiders loot the church, carrying off large gold crosses and precious candlesticks. They rip silken cloths from the walls and pull wooden statues from their bases. Lustily singing and laughing, the Vikings race down the beach, pile the slaves and treasure into their ships, and sail away.

ost of what we know of the Lindisfarne raid comes from the Anglo-Saxon Chronicle, written by an unknown author about a hundred years after the event. Scholars generally consider this attack on Lindisfarne to be the start of the Viking Age. Over the following three centuries, Vikings from Scandinavia—

Raiders advance with upraised swords and battle-axes in this memorial gravestone from the tenth century, which depicts the Viking attack on the monastery at Lindisfarne in 793.

the modern countries of Denmark, Norway, and Sweden—sailed their majestic ships to many parts of Europe, Asia, and even North America.

Many Viking adventurers went to raid and to loot. But Viking merchants also traveled abroad, trading Scandinavian articles for goods from other lands. Still other Vikings explored new lands, sought new places to settle, and founded new communities. From the Lindisfarne attack and the many other attacks that followed arose the popular—though now disputed—belief that all Vikings were cruel, ruthless pirates and murderers.

Archaeologists have recently uncovered many remains from the Viking Age, the period from around 800 to 1100, that give a more balanced view of Viking life than previously held. As experts dig in the places where Vikings lived, they are finding many everyday objects preserved in the soil. These include coins and silver jewelry, carved animal bones, furniture, clothing, boots, and weapons. Archaeologists are also uncovering the foundations of buildings and the remains of large ships.

A dig in what is now Dublin, Ireland, revealed the wooden planks of a Viking road and the remains of houses and shops. This animal horn found at the site may have been used to practice carving designs.

The carved inscription around the border of this memorial stone is written in the Viking system of letters and symbols known as runes. It reads: "Gufi raised this stone in memory of Olafr, his son, a very good valiant man. He was killed in Estonia." The name of the stonecutter is also included. According to Viking legend, the runic alphabet (below) was a gift from the great god Odin. Some rune stones were painted with bright colors. Sometimes only the carved lines were painted.

f u th ą r k h n i a s t b m l R

From studies of these finds, scholars have learned that the majority of Viking Age Scandinavians did not go out raiding. Instead, most of them stayed home, where they farmed, raised cattle, and hunted and fished. Some built ships. Viking craftsmen produced a variety of goods in their workshops. Viking merchants traveled widely, trading these goods for materials from other lands.

Evidence from Viking graves tells us about everyday life. Some men and women were buried with their most valuable possessions and occasionally with their horses and dogs. Some people were buried in fine wooden ships or within enclosures of stones arranged in boat shapes. The ship settings suggest that the Vikings thought that death was followed by a voyage to the next world.

Clues to Viking life and beliefs also come from their ancestral histories and heroic legends, which families once passed on by word of mouth. On long, dark, cold winter evenings in Viking lands, family elders repeated these stories, sometimes known as sagas, again and again. Later, long after the end of the Viking Age, scribes wrote down the sagas. Among the most famous tales are *Egil's Saga, Erik the Red's Saga,* and *The Greenlanders' Saga,* all of which people still enjoy reading.

The few written records left by the Vikings consist of inscriptions on gravestones, road markers, weapons, and jewelry. The Vikings wrote in letters called runes, which also served as magic symbols. The 16 letters of the runic alphabet were angular in shape, which made them easy to carve into hard surfaces, such as stone or metal. Although many runic stones were memorials to dead relatives, other inscriptions marked property boundaries, noted important events, or offered thanks to a god.

From archaeological excavations, sagas, runes, and the writings of their enemies and victims, we've learned much about the Vikings, a people who triumphed over the cold and isolation of their homelands to forge a distinctive culture and destiny.

Egil Skallagrimsson, the hero of *Egil's Saga,* stands with sword at hand. A tenth-century Icelander, Egil embodied both sides of the Viking character. According to the saga, he was tough and cruel, but at the same time he won fame as a merchant, farmer, and great poet.

CHAPTER TWO

AT HOME IN SCANDINAVIA

Hedeby, a large, important town in Viking times, is the most thoroughly explored of all Viking sites. From remains that archaeologists have uncovered there, we have a fairly good idea of what a Viking town looked like and of how ordinary people lived there.

Both a fort and a trading center, Hedeby is located at the southeast corner of Denmark, facing the Baltic Sea. In Viking times, a high wall of earth surrounded the town. In some places the wall was 40 feet tall—the height of a four-story building. People had to walk through tunnels in the wall to get in or out of Hedeby. A small brook ran through the center of the town, providing the residents with water for drinking and washing.

Hedeby had at least two main streets, both paved with planks of wood. Most houses were built of wattle and daub—flexible willow branches threaded in and out of posts and covered with mud and cow dung. Wealthy people lived in wooden houses built from tree trunks, which were split lengthwise and placed upright in the ground to form a continuous wall. Other houses were made with wooden planks placed horizontally. Covering the houses were roofs of reed thatching or sod—thick, matted grass growing in a thin layer of earth. Behind each house was an outhouse, a well, a cesspool, and a pit for garbage.

Rich merchants and craftsmen in Hedeby lived in large wooden houses that measured about 16 by 40 feet. The living room had a central fireplace with a cooking pot hanging over the hearth. The fireplace provided both heat and light. A small hole in the roof let the smoke out. Low earth platforms, built up on both sides of the fireplace, served as benches for sitting and sleeping.

The houses had no windows. Light came from the fireplace or from lamps, which were

Reconstructions of ninth-century buildings, these houses are found in Hedeby, Denmark, once the largest Viking town. A busy trading center, Hedeby had a population of about 1,000 to 1,500 people in Viking times.

In this scene of a Viking home, a woman dresses her child while another stirs a cooking pot over a hearth. The fire provides both heat and light. The hole in the roof allows smoke to escape and serves as another source of light for the windowless house. A bird's-eye view of Hedeby, Denmark (below), shows the many houses crowded together, the farms on the outskirts of town, and the sea. A high wall of earth surrounds the town, for protection.

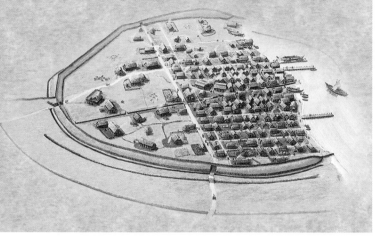

Ⱥ Viking woman used this carved whalebone board and heavy green glass smoother to keep her family's clothes neatly pressed.

small iron or soapstone bowls holding wicks, probably made of plant fibers, for burning oil. Still, it must have been dark indoors—as well as smelly and smoky—so many tasks were probably done outside.

The wattle-and-daub huts of the poorer people of Hedeby were about 9 by 12 feet. They had a fireplace in one corner and earthen benches along the walls.

From objects found at Hedeby, it appears that many of the townspeople worked as merchants and craftsmen. Some of the craftsmen made jewelry. Others were expert glassblowers, who produced everything from glass beads for necklaces to drinking cups. Some craftsmen carved

Perched amid metalworking tools, a delicate animal ornament reflects the artistry of a Viking jeweler. Viking craftsmen used molds, such as the dragon's head mold at left, to produce a variety of metal objects.

objects of horn or bone. Still others made their living weaving and sewing cloth.

Archaeologists have found two important tools that Viking craftsmen used to make marvelous objects from metal: the crucible and the mold. The crucible, a pot of hard-fired clay, allowed workers to melt metal at very high temperatures before shaping it. Molds, also made of clay, made it possible to easily produce a great many objects, from pots to rings to battle-axes to statues.

Viking merchants brought fine goods from Germany, France, England, Constantinople, and Persia to trade in Hedeby. Indeed, people from all over Scandinavia visited the town's bustling market to buy jewelry, silk, lace, and other luxuries. Slaves captured on raids were also traded at Hedeby.

Based on the excavation of Vorbasse, Denmark, this diagram shows the layout of a typical Viking farming village. The longhouses on each farm sheltered Viking families as well as their livestock. Farmers used iron sheep shears and wool combs (bottom, right) to produce wool for home use and for trade. Horse-drawn carts, shown in the picture stone at bottom, left, were used for transportation.

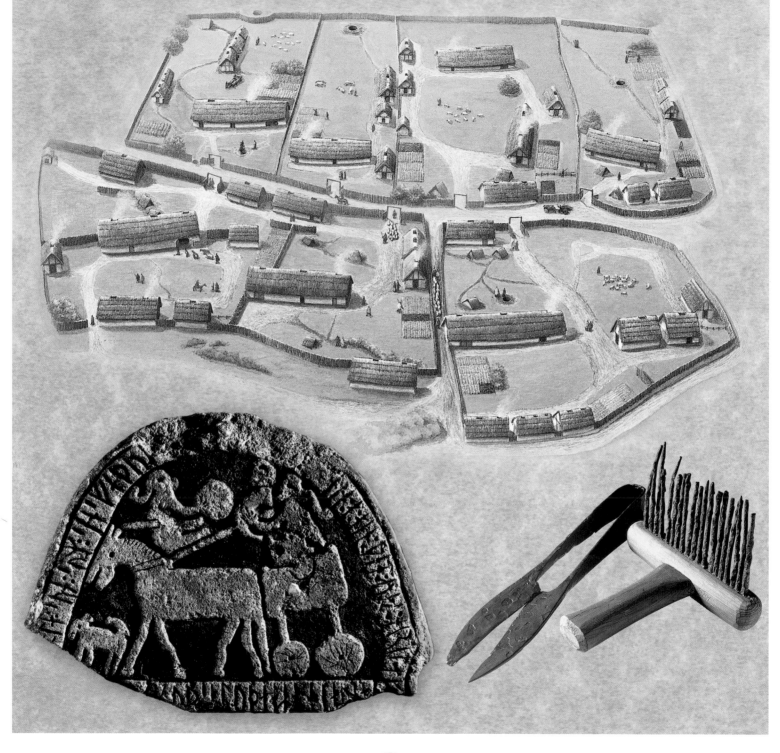

While some Vikings lived in towns such as Hedeby, most people were farmers in the countryside. A typical farm contained the family house, stables and barns for the farm animals, a workshop to make metal tools, and small huts for slaves. Farms on the coast usually had a shed to hold the farmer's boat during the winter months.

Farmers raised mainly corn, peas, cabbage, barley, and oats. They kept cattle both for meat and for milk. The farmers' wives churned the milk into butter or made cheese, which they kept in cold storerooms, using the winter snow as a kind of deep freeze. They also pickled and smoked meat and stored dried peas and beans. Without these preserved foods, the people would have had nothing to eat during the winter.

Every member of a farm family shared in the work. Men worked the fields, hunted and fished, and looked after the livestock. Women preserved and cooked the food, cared for the children and the sick, spun and wove wool, and sewed, embroidered, and washed clothes. They ran the farm while their husbands and sons were away fishing or on trading or raiding voyages—sometimes for months or years at a time. Children helped their parents around the house and farm. Even the youngest ones contributed by feeding the animals or gathering firewood.

Viking family groups were large. A man and his wife, their children—including older sons with their wives and children—and the grandparents all lived together on the family farm. When a daughter married, she usually left home to join her husband's family.

Vikings ate two main meals a day. The women served the first meal at about eight or nine o'clock in the morning, which was after the farmers had already worked in the fields for about two hours. The other meal, which they ate at about seven or eight o'clock in the evening, marked the end of the day's work.

At dinner, members of the family sat around the table, sometimes on the same benches they slept on at night. They ate off rectangular wooden platters or from soapstone bowls, using only spoons and knives, which they carried in their belts. Forks were a later invention.

In good times, Viking families supped on soups and stews of beef or mutton or on fish from the sea. Women roasted meat on huge spits over the hearth and cooked vegetables in big iron cauldrons. They baked bread in stone ovens or on long-handled flat metal griddles placed on the ashes of the fire.

For drinks, the children and women had cow's, sheep's, or goat's milk—usually just the whey, or buttermilk. They also drank juice squeezed from berries.

The usual drink for men was mead, a sweet alcoholic brew made from honey. They drank from drinking horns as well as cups. Since the horns did not have flat bottoms, drinkers could not set them down without spilling until the horns were completely empty. A person had to drink all the mead in the horn or else pass it to the others around the table until the drink was finished. Vikings admired a man who could drain a drinking horn in one gulp.

When not working, Vikings played games such as chess and went swimming and skiing. A board game called *merils*, which is similar to checkers, has been found in Viking graves. Other recreational activities included fencing, running, and wrestling, as well as training falcons to hunt wild birds and animals.

Drink was often served in large ox horns that were hollowed out and polished. After a toast, each man was expected to finish his drink before the horn was refilled. Sometimes two people shared a horn.

Vikings slid across frozen rivers and lakes on skates carved from polished horse or cattle bones. Below, a skater pushes off with an iron-tipped pole, a common method of skating in Viking times.

Carved from walrus tusks, these ivory chess pieces date back to 12th-century Norway. Viking men enjoyed playing chess since it was based on war games and involved protecting the king from attack.

Winter sports included racing on snow-shoes and ice-skating. Skates were made of sharpened animal bones attached to shoes with leather straps. Skaters used long, sharpened poles to push themselves on the ice. In warmer weather, ball games were popular.

The Vikings were fond of music. They celebrated victories and festivals in song, which might be accompanied by harps or lyres. From findings at various archaeological sites, we know that the Vikings also had simple wind instruments. Pipes unearthed in Sweden were made of hollowed-out animal bones, with holes drilled along the length to produce the different tones.

If a girl wanted to marry into a good family, she had to be able to sing and play an instrument. Boys also had to be musical, but they needed to master other skills as well, especially the use of weapons. One young Viking man boasted:

"There are nine skills known to me—
At the chessboard I am skillful,
Runic writing I know well,
Books I like; with tools am handy,
Good with snowshoes,
rowing, and shooting,
And expert with harp and verse."

Life was hard in Viking times—but there was obviously still time to relax and have fun.

CHAPTER THREE

VIKING KINGS AND GODS

At the beginning of the Viking Age, the lands of Scandinavia were divided into many small, separate kingdoms. These domains were often at war, with each leader trying to capture another's land.

Kings and powerful chieftains built forts to provide living quarters for soldiers and their families. These forts soon became places where craftsmen worked and merchants traded goods. For protection, the forts were usually surrounded by a mound of earth with a tall, wooden fence on top and a deep ditch on the outside. Four such fortifications have been excavated in Denmark. Parts of an especially long fortification, the Danevirke, which marked the southern boundary of Denmark, still stand today.

In Viking times, a king's oldest son did not automatically become king on the death of his father. He could ascend the throne only by proving that he was a good leader or by battling other aspiring nobles. Small wonder that King Magnus Barelegs of Norway said, "A king is for glory, not for long life." In fact, Magnus was slain at the young age of 30.

Gradually, the more powerful kings of Scandinavia took over the territories of their weaker neighbors. By about 1050, only three kings remained, ruling over three countries: Denmark, Norway, and Sweden.

Below the kings in rank were the most powerful and wealthy Vikings, called *jarls* (related to the English word "earls"). These men owned large estates in the countryside and often recruited armies and built their own forts. Jarls displayed their great wealth by offering their subjects generous meals and vast quantities of drink at special festivals honoring the gods or

Odin was the king of the Viking gods. Also known as Wotan, Woden, or Wodan, the supernatural being was revered as a fearless fighter, a powerful seer, and a brilliant poet. This manuscript illustration shows Odin as he is usually portrayed, holding a sword, with two meat-eating ravens perched on his shoulders. According to a Viking legend, Odin lost his right eye when he went to drink water from the well of wisdom, which was guarded by the giant Mimir. When Mimir demanded one of Odin's eyes as payment, Odin plucked it out without hesitation. From drinking at the well, Odin gained complete knowledge of the past, present, and future.

Found in Norway, the brass keys below were functional as well as ornamental. Such keys usually hung from a woman's belt. They indicated her control over the farm and the storage chests where valuables were kept. Viking women usually wore long wool or linen dresses with woolen tunics that looked like aprons. Buckles or brooches, such as this gold one from Denmark, were used to fasten the shoulder straps of their garments. A Viking jeweler adorned this brooch with filigree, fine gold wire applied to the surface to look like strings of tiny beads, often in an intricate pattern.

celebrating a good harvest or successful raid. Such celebrations could last for days.

Most people in Viking society were *karls,* or freemen. Some karls were merchants, fishermen, trappers, or craft workers. But the majority were farmers who worked the land, although they sometimes went on raids or other adventures. Most karls willingly followed their jarl into battle in distant lands.

Karls used *thralls,* or slaves, as laborers on their farms or ships or in their workshops. Thralls had few rights. Their owners had the power of life and death over them. The children of thralls were thralls as well.

Viking women did not have equal rights with men, but they were not entirely powerless. Viking women could own property and share the wealth of their husbands. They could also divorce their husbands at will.

People measured a woman's wealth by the jewelry she wore. Viking women fastened their cloaks and kerchiefs with massive gold or silver clasps, called brooches. (The Vikings did not have buttons.) Females and males alike adorned themselves with gold and silver finger rings and arm bracelets. A man's jewelry was often a gift from a king or other noble, awarded to him for bold and brave deeds.

All early Vikings, from kings to thralls, worshiped many gods. They believed that these gods dwelled in Viking heaven, known as Asgard. Within Asgard was an elegant hall called Valhalla. People believed that brave fighters slain in battle would be carried off to Valhalla by beautiful princesses known as Valkyries. The Valkyries were said to ride their horses across the sky, collecting the bodies of brave warriors who had been killed in battle. Once in Valhalla, the men fought all day without suffering wounds, and they drank and feasted all night without getting drunk or sick.

At death, ordinary people went to a different realm, known as Niflheim, also called Hel. Though not a pleasant place, Hel was not nearly as terrible as the Christian hell is thought to be. But for most Vikings, leading a good life and achieving lasting fame in this world mattered more than the afterlife.

The Vikings thought that Odin, king of the gods, rode through the sky on his eight-legged horse, Sleipnir. Wise, cunning, and dangerous, Odin was also the god of battle, who

In Viking lore, maidens called Valkyries (top left) welcomed slain warriors to Valhalla (above). Valhalla had 540 doors, to admit many warriors at once. The figurine at left depicts the god Odin.

In this modern-day painted carving at Town Hall in Oslo, Norway, Odin rides his eight-legged horse, Sleipnir, across the sky. Passionately devoted to Odin, Viking warriors known as berserkers were notorious for their wild and frenzied combat. Some were said to chew on their shields before battle, as depicted in the ivory chess piece at left.

brought victory to his followers. Among these followers were a class of wild warriors called berserkers. Inspired by Odin, they rushed madly into battle, shrieking and leaping, sometimes naked. From their frenzied behavior comes the English word "berserk."

One Viking myth dealing with Odin appears in a 13th-century collection of poems known as the *Poetic Edda.* In the myth, Odin hangs himself "for nine whole nights, / Upon a windswept tree" to gain wisdom. As a result, Odin could raise the dead and see into the future.

Poets, who had important roles as chroniclers of Viking life, drew inspiration from Odin, who was said to recite wonderful poetry himself. He was also known as Woden, a name that has given us the word "Wednesday." Odin's wife was Frigg. "Friday," from "Frigg's day," is named after her.

Odin was king of the gods, but powerful, red-bearded Thor was undoubtedly the most popular Viking god. Legends describe Thor as a fighter of great size and strength. When he crossed the heavens in his enormous chariot, thunder and lightning struck the Earth. Thor's symbol was a hammer that represented a thunderbolt. Many Viking men wore a carving of Thor's hammer on a leather thong around their necks as protection against evil spirits. "Thursday," from "Thor's day," became the usual time to hold meetings and great feasts.

People praised Thor for slaying the evil World Serpent. Thor controlled the weather, so seafarers prayed to him for safe voyages, and farmers pleaded for good crops. People also considered Thor the upholder of the laws and dispenser of justice, swearing oaths in his name.

The twins Frey and Freya were the god and goddess of love and fertility. Frey blessed marriages and the births of children and animals. When farmers sowed their crops they scattered bread and poured wine onto the ground to please Frey, so he would make the crops grow tall and hardy. People also believed that Freya welcomed women who had died in childbirth into the next world.

Instead of praying in churches or temples, the Vikings usually worshiped outdoors. People also occasionally came together for ceremonies in their chieftains' great halls. These public devotions took place in addition to the usual day-to-day religious rituals observed by each family.

Thor, depicted at right, was the god of storms, thunder, and strength. In this tenth-century figurine, his beard is transformed into his hammer. Vikings believed that the sound of thunder came from Thor striking a foe with the mighty tool. According to legend, Thor caught the evil World Serpent by baiting a hook with the head of an ox (above).

A modern-day town nestles at the base of a Norwegian fjord, which is a narrow inlet of the sea between high cliffs (left). Many Vikings lived around fjords, which were good starting points for their fishing trips and other voyages. The town of Hedeby, pictured above in wintertime, was a meeting place for merchants and settlers, who gathered to buy and sell animals, fruits and vegetables, cloth, glass, weapons, tools, furs, and slaves.

Survival was a continuing concern for the Vikings. Their biggest problem was growing enough to eat. Much of their land was rough woods and mountains. Winters were long and harsh, with snow and freezing conditions lasting for many months. Summers could be warm and sunny, but they were short and provided little time for raising food crops successfully. Periodic shortages of fish in the waters around Viking lands added to the constant danger of starvation. During times of scarcity, few had enough to eat and drink, and many people died.

Viking kings and jarls harshly punished those who refused to serve them and obey their laws. The punishments ranged from fines to stonings to declaring the offenders to be outlaws. Outlaws were stripped of all their lands and possessions. Feuds between families, with killings on both sides, were very common. Indeed, the slightest argument or insult could set one group against another. Such feuds often carried on from generation to generation.

Negative conditions such as these influenced many Vikings to take to the sea. From the 780s onward, untold numbers of Vikings ventured throughout Europe—westward to what is now Britain and France and eastward across what is now Russia. The Viking raiders, traders, and settlers became the leading seafarers of the world. Everywhere they went, they brought about major changes, some of which are still with us today.

CHAPTER FOUR

THE VIKING ADVANTAGE

Before Viking times, Scandinavians built strong, sturdy boats that were neither very fast nor large. All lacked sails and were hard to control. By the end of the ninth century, everything had changed. The Vikings had invented better ships, and they were sweeping across Europe in them.

Striking evidence of Viking shipbuilding skill was discovered in 1880, when archaeologists opened a large burial mound at Gokstad, Norway. Inside they found the well-preserved remains of a longship built sometime between the years 850 and 900. The discovery of the Gokstad ship was one of the most exciting breakthroughs of Viking archaeology. This ship was one of the first to reveal how the Vikings built the large, fast ships that made their long voyages possible.

The Vikings improved the old vessels in several ways. Perhaps most important, they introduced large sails, which were woven of wool and colored with a pattern of bright squares. Some sails stretched as much as 40 feet across. In general, Viking sailors hoisted a ship's sail in open seas. They learned how to sail either with, across, or against the wind. During storms, the mariners spread out the sail like a tent to protect themselves. When there was no wind, or when they were navigating along narrow rivers, the Vikings used oars to power their ships.

The Vikings were among the first to use a keel, a long, narrow strip of wood that runs down the center of a ship's underside. The keel adds to a ship's stability. They also found a very efficient way of steering. One man stood at the right side of the rear, or stern, of the ship, holding an oar that was fixed to the ship's side. By pushing the oar in one direction or another, he steered the ship. The oar was called the steerboard. From it comes the English word "starboard," which means the right side of a ship.

Lashing down their goods and weapons, Viking merchant-plunderers ride out a storm at sea. Viking vessels, such as this cargo ship, handled well even in rough seas. A strong keel helped the ship stay stable, while a fixed oar, or steerboard, made it easy to maneuver.

Viking sailors learned to navigate by observing the stars, the flight of birds, or even the smell of sheep when they were nearing land.

The Vikings built the hulls of their ships of overlapping planks of oak. They nailed the planks together and tied them to the ribs of the ships with strands of animal hair or spruce root. This mode of construction allowed the ships to bend and twist in the water without

A 1904 excavation of a queen's burial mound in Oseberg, Norway, reveals a well-preserved Viking ship. Ninth-century Vikings buried their monarch in the vessel, along with food, furniture, clothes, farm and kitchen tools, a wagon, and a sled.

breaking. By stuffing the joints with rope, yarn, and tar, the builders made the ships watertight.

These shipbuilding techniques enabled the vessels to ride over the waves rather than plow through them. The ships could sail at high speeds and weather ferocious ocean storms. They could also travel on rivers as shallow as three feet deep.

When archaeologists removed the Gokstad longship from the clay bed that had protected it in the ground, they found that the ship's overall length was 76 1/2 feet, with a width of 17 1/2 feet at the middle. This is about as long as a

tennis court and nearly as wide. The tall mast was attached to a hinge set in the ship's bottom. This allowed the sailors to raise or lower the mast.

Although the Gokstad ship had a sail, it could also be rowed with oars. There were 16 oars on each side. The oar holes had hinged disks on the inside that the sailors closed when not in use. Since there were no fixed benches, the oarsmen most likely sat on their own sea chests while rowing.

The Gokstad ship had a row of shields, black and yellow in color, along either side. These beautiful shields were probably displayed only when the ship was at anchor.

Viking sailors also used trading ships, known as *knarrs,* for carrying cargo and settlers to and from new lands. At 53 feet, the knarrs were shorter than the longships. But their deep bodies made them ideal for storing supplies and shipping people, goods, and animals across the seas. The first knarr ever found intact was unearthed in 1962.

Modern boatbuilders have made several reconstructions of old Viking ships. Sailors have used them to retrace some of the journeys of the ancient Vikings. Above all, these voyages have proved one thing—that the great successes of the Viking raiders, traders, and settlers depended on their extraordinary ships.

The Gokstad longship (left) was the first complete Viking ship ever discovered. A longship contrasts with a knarr in the diagram at top. A typical Viking anchor, nearly 10 feet wide, was made of wood weighted down by a large rock.

Viking warriors carried wooden shields (left) held together with strong iron nails. In the center is a large, dome-shaped piece of iron called a boss, which protected the warrior's hand. Shields were sometimes painted with elaborate designs. The double-edged slashing swords below belonged to wealthy Viking chieftains. Their richly ornamented handles are decorated with gold or silver.

iking weapons, while not as innovative as their magnificent sailing ships, were equally well made. Warriors had to provide their own weapons and armor for battle. These included a shield for defense, as well as attack weapons such as swords, spears, battle-axes, and clubs. Bows and arrows were also used in battle. Rich Vikings sometimes rode horses to the battlefield or brought them to foreign lands by ship. But they did not fight on horseback.

Most fighting consisted of hand-to-hand combat, with the favored weapons being swords, spears, and battle-axes. Wielded by a powerful warrior, a heavy sword or ax could crash through a shield and slay an enemy with one blow.

Wealthy Vikings spent huge sums on weapons that were often decorated with runes and magical designs. Karls passed down favorite swords, sharpened on both sides, from father to son and gave them names such as Fire of Battle, Leg-Biter, or Long and Sharp.

Spears were either light or heavy. Lighter ones were used for throwing; heavier spears were thrust at opponents. After a victory in battle, soldiers collected the weapons and armor from dead enemies and distributed them among the triumphant fighters.

Many Vikings charged into battle with no more protection than thick layers of animal hides sewed onto their long tunics. Usually only the chieftains wore metal-link armor and leather or metal helmets.

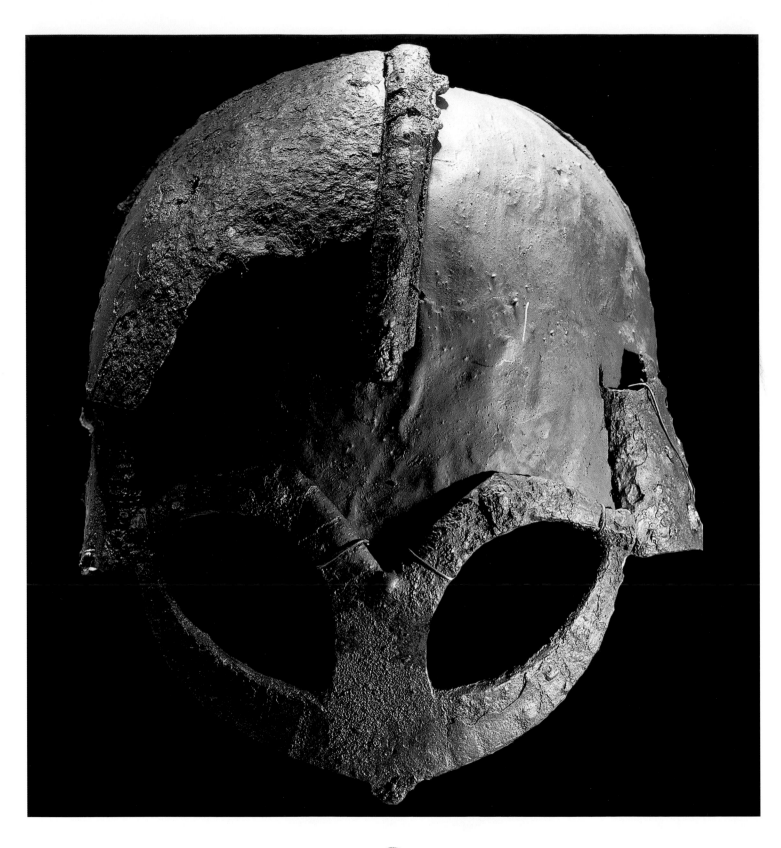

oder, almost all representations of Viking helmets show them with cattle horns on the sides. But of all the remains of Viking helmets that have been found, and in all accounts of Viking warrior dress, there are no hints of horns. The horn idea actually arose near the middle of the 19th century, when German composer Richard Wagner wrote several operas based on old Viking legends, and the costume designer dressed the characters in horned helmets.

Viking ships and weapons represent the best examples of fine craftsmanship in those times. Both were tools of conquest, as well as objects of great beauty.

Before the Viking Age, the peoples of Scandinavia had seaworthy boats. But none could compare with the Viking ships for speed, size, or navigability. Viking vessels were flexible and strong—able to sail through the roughest seas without breaking apart. The warriors' long, sharp swords were supple enough to withstand the most powerful blows. Together, these advantages helped make possible the Vikings' far-ranging voyages and many military conquests.

A souvenir in a Norwegian shop reflects the popular idea that Vikings wore horn-sprouting helmets (right). In truth, Vikings wore simple helmets, such as the tenth-century example at left, which was reconstructed from fragments found in the grave of a Viking chieftain in Norway.

CHAPTER FIVE

SWEEPING ACROSS EUROPE

Vikings from different homelands embarked on their trading or raiding adventures in different regions of Europe. Vikings from Norway favored Scotland and the Scottish Islands, Ireland, and northwest England. Danish Vikings looted and burned dozens of towns in England, Germany, the Netherlands, and France. The Swedes mostly swept over Russia and lands to the east and south.

At the beginning of the ninth century, the land that is now known as England was divided into a number of kingdoms. By the end of the century, Danish Vikings controlled most of them. As the Vikings raided and swept through much of England, they frequently forced the English to pay them large sums of money, called *danegeld* ("Danish money"), to secure their lands from attack.

Led by the Viking chieftain Guthrum, the Danes succeeded in conquering a large part of England. This area became known as the Danelaw because it was subject to the laws of the Danes. Guthrum was crowned its king.

The city of York was taken over by the Vikings in 867. Under Viking control, it became a major center for trade and crafts.

Excavations in modern York have turned up Viking coins, ruins of Viking buildings, and other evidence of a Viking presence, including knives that still slice and ice skates of bone that still work perfectly well on frozen ponds. Archaeologists today picture a town with many Viking merchants and craftsmen practicing bone carving, leather working, and metalcraft.

Most Vikings spoke the same language, which is now known as Old Norse. The names of some of the streets in modern-day York can be traced back to their Old Norse origins: Skeldergate (from the word for "shield") was once a center for shield makers. Coppergate (from the word for "barrelmakers")

Well-armed Danish raiders approach the English coast in 866 in this illustration from a 12th-century English manuscript. In the battle that followed, the Viking warriors, led by Ivar the Boneless, defeated the English and went on to conquer more than half of England.

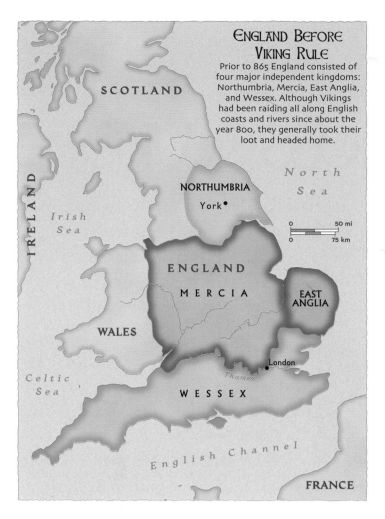

England Before Viking Rule

Prior to 865 England consisted of four major independent kingdoms: Northumbria, Mercia, East Anglia, and Wessex. Although Vikings had been raiding all along English coasts and rivers since about the year 800, they generally took their loot and headed home.

SCOTLAND

IRELAND

Irish Sea

North Sea

NORTHUMBRIA

York

0   50 mi
0   75 km

ENGLAND

MERCIA

EAST ANGLIA

WALES

Celtic Sea

London

Thames

WESSEX

English Channel

FRANCE

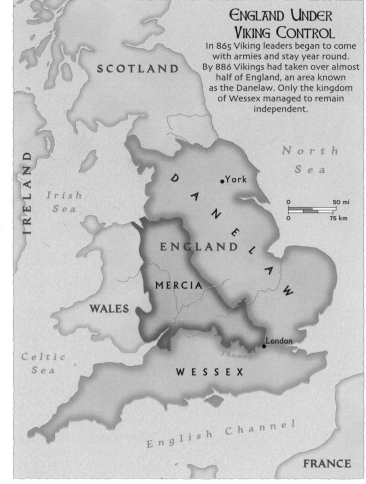

England Under Viking Control

In 865 Viking leaders began to come with armies and stay year round. By 886 Vikings had taken over almost half of England, an area known as the Danelaw. Only the kingdom of Wessex managed to remain independent.

SCOTLAND

IRELAND

Irish Sea

North Sea

DANELAW

York

0   50 mi
0   75 km

ENGLAND

MERCIA

WALES

Celtic Sea

London

Thames

WESSEX

English Channel

FRANCE

was the name for the woodworkers' area.

Around 878, the Danes attacked King Alfred of Wessex, leader of the last independent kingdom. King Alfred and his armies resisted Guthrum's attacks, however, and Wessex remained independent.

The Vikings controlled the Danelaw until the death of Erik Bloodaxe, the last Viking king of the area, in 954. During the time it was under Viking rule, many Viking families settled in the Danelaw and became farmers.

Starting in 845, the city of Paris, France, was a frequent target of Viking raids. Although it was protected by stone walls, the walls did not always keep out the Vikings. They took away everything of value they could carry, stole food crops and livestock, and captured men and women to use as slaves or to return in exchange for ransom.

Around the year 885, Viking fighters again laid siege to Paris, this time in a year-long campaign. The king finally gave the Vikings

Vikings assault Paris on the Île de la Cité, an island in the Seine River. They attacked in 885 after being refused free passage up the river.

a huge treasury to end the fighting. In 911, the Vikings were back. The French king, Charles III, known as Charles the Fat, invited the Viking chieftain Rollo to sign a treaty agreeing to protect France from all future Viking invasions. In return, Charles gave Rollo control of a northern part of the country now known as Normandy, a word that comes partly from Northmen, or Vikings.

Rome was another great city targeted by Vikings. In 859, the Viking chieftain Hastein set out from Paris and sailed his fleet of 62 ships along the coasts of France, Portugal, and Spain, pillaging and looting at every stop. The Vikings then dipped down to the coast of Africa and captured many black African men to sell as slaves.

According to an account by the monk Dudo of St. Quentin, the Viking forces eventually reached a gleaming white city inland from the Italian coast. Hastein thought he had arrived at Rome, but it was probably Luna, about 100 miles to the north.

Much to Hastein's surprise, a huge, well-equipped army stood ready to defend the city. Realizing that he could not overwhelm the enemy by force, Hastein resorted to trickery. Pretending to be dying, he sent messengers ashore asking that he be baptized as a Christian. The bishop agreed to let the men bring Hastein to the church. After the blessing, Hastein rejoined his troops.

The next day, messengers again deceived the bishop, saying that Hastein had died during the night. The bishop consented to hold a funeral Mass and church burial for the dead Viking leader.

Back on his ship, the fully armed Hastein lay down in a coffin while his attendants hid weapons and armor under their clothes. Then the army of Vikings carried the coffin to the church. When the funeral Mass was over, Hastein flung back the coffin lid and sprang to his feet. With a swift blow, he killed the flabbergasted bishop. After pillaging the church, the raiders ransacked the entire city.

Archaeologists have found no evidence that these events actually occurred. But all experts agree that Hastein never reached Rome. He did sail on to Alexandria, Egypt, before returning to Paris in 862. Reportedly, only 20 of his 62 ships survived the voyage.

Viking warriors battle their eastern foes in territory that is now Russia, in this scene from an Icelandic saga.

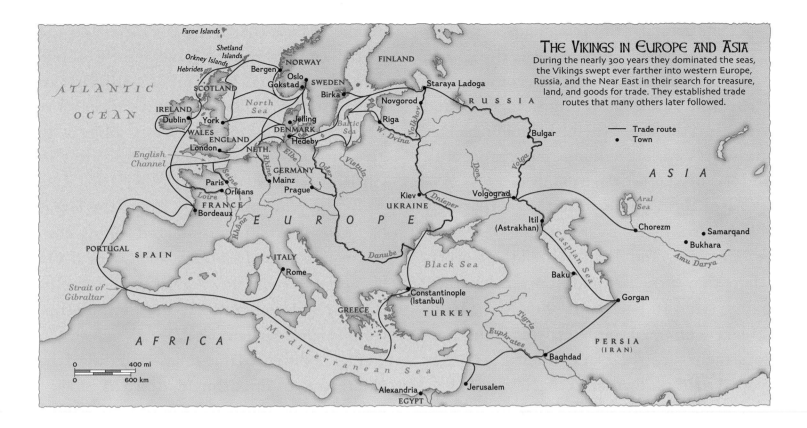

THE VIKINGS IN EUROPE AND ASIA

During the nearly 300 years they dominated the seas, the Vikings swept ever farther into western Europe, Russia, and the Near East in their search for treasure, land, and goods for trade. They established trade routes that many others later followed.

For the most part, Swedish Vikings headed east, using the Baltic Sea as a highway for ships bound for Russia. They also traveled inland along the rivers, following the Dnieper to the Black Sea and the Volga to the Caspian Sea.

Many Swedish Vikings raided towns and villages along the coasts and rivers of Russia, attacking any weak settlements. Scholars believe, however, that more Swedes went to Russia as traders and settlers than as raiders. Large numbers of these Vikings stayed, built homes, and settled in such towns as Kiev and Novgorod, turning them into busy trading centers with large populations. Some Swedish Vikings ventured even farther, traveling on foot or by camel beyond where the rivers ended to reach the Middle Eastern cities of Baghdad and Jerusalem.

Many of the native peoples in the regions where the Swedish Vikings settled were Slavs. They called the Swedes "Rus," which possibly gave the name "Russia" to the area. By the middle years of the tenth century, the Rus had taken on many Slavic customs. The Swedish Vikings even adopted Slav or Central Asian dress, such as a helmet with a pointed tip and baggy trousers gathered at the knees.

The great age of Viking raids was nearly over by the end of the tenth century. The Viking kings were becoming more powerful, building up mighty armies and increasing the size of their land holdings. This meant less warfare at home, more prosperity, and less need for foreign goods.

Also, the Vikings found it increasingly difficult to attack the various lands of Europe. Strong armies and fleets awaited them everywhere they turned. In addition, many Vikings had settled in the lands they had earlier attacked. Some of these settlers had become so attached to their new homes that they helped fight off further Viking invasions.

During the 10th and 11th centuries Viking culture changed in many ways. Perhaps most important was that Vikings gradually gave up their belief in pagan gods and came to accept Christianity, which was the dominant religion in the rest of Europe.

The work of Christian missionaries from England and Germany was largely responsible for the Viking conversions. The missionaries traveled throughout Viking lands, building churches and urging the people to base their religious beliefs on the Christian teachings of Jesus and the Bible. The Viking kings were among the first to convert to Christianity. Then, by force or by persuasion, the kings got their subjects to give up their pagan practices and pray in Christian churches.

By the year 1016, King Canute the Great had extended and consolidated Viking control over Norway, Denmark, and England. On his death in 1042, however, several different earls and jarls fought to succeed him and control the lands he had ruled.

Out of the chaos that followed, Edward the Confessor, an Englishman, arose as king of England. When he died in 1066 leaving no heir, another Englishman, Harold Godwinson, took over as the new English king.

In the fall of that same year, the Norwegian king Harald Hardrada attacked England with some 300 ships and 9,000 warriors. Despite this great effort, Harald was soundly defeated by King Harold Godwinson at the Battle of Stamford Bridge.

While King Harold Godwinson was crushing the Norwegians,

Old beliefs meet new in the tenth-century Viking pendant at left, which combines Thor's hammer with a Christian cross. Found in a tenth-century grave in Sweden, the silver crucifix at right is the oldest known Viking image of Christ.

King Harold Godwinson of England lies slain as his troops face defeat by William the Conqueror's cavalry in this engraving of the Battle of Hastings. Two months after the battle, William was crowned king of England on Christmas Day, 1066.

Duke William of Normandy—later known as William the Conqueror—invaded England by crossing the English Channel from what is now France. William himself was of Viking descent. His great-great-grandfather was the chieftain Rollo, who had forced the French to give the Vikings control of Normandy.

King Harold rushed south to confront William, and the two forces met at the Battle of Hastings, where Harold was killed. William was then crowned king of England. Most experts agree that the ascension of William the Conqueror to the English throne in 1066 marks the end of the Viking Age.

CHAPTER SIX

CROSSING THE ATLANTIC

Until the late ninth century, most Viking trading and raiding voyages were centered in Europe. As time went on, however, the Vikings ventured farther west into the North Atlantic Ocean.

The Vikings' first important land discovery was the result of an accident. Two men, a Swede named Gardar Svavarson and a Norwegian known only as Naddod, were sailing separately toward islands near Scotland in the year 860. They were both blown off course and landed on an unknown island about a thousand miles west of Scandinavia.

Gardar, proud of his finding, named the new land "Gardar's Isle." Naddod, seeing the coastal waters still choked with ice in the middle of spring, gave the place a more descriptive name: "Snowland," or "Iceland." When they returned to their homes in Scandinavia, both men told vivid stories of a foreign land covered with green pastures and full of game and fish. Yet, despite their fantastic claims, no one else explored Iceland for another ten years.

In the year 870, Ingolf Arnason of Norway was forced to flee his native country after a family feud in which he killed two sons of a noble jarl. Ingolf headed for Iceland, hoping to settle in this new territory. After a difficult crossing, he arrived in two ships with some followers, a number of Irish slaves, and a few seasick livestock.

As he neared the shores of Iceland, Ingolf cast overboard two wooden pillars that he had brought with him from his home in Norway. Following an old Viking ritual, he vowed that he would establish his colony at the place where the pillars drifted ashore. Meanwhile he set up camp near his landing site.

It took three years before the pillars swept onto the sand of a sheltered bay on the southwest coast of Iceland. Ingolf named

Towering icebergs and curious sea creatures greet Erik the Red as he arrives in Greenland around the year 982. Attracted by the land's grassy slopes, many wild animals, and plentiful fishing, Erik later brought settlers over from Iceland and laid claim to the land in 985.

Clouds of steam rising from hot springs near Reykjavík must have surprised the first Viking settlers in Iceland.

the spot Reykjavík, meaning "steamy bay," because of the vapor rising from nearby hot springs. Here Ingolf built his house and started his farm. Excavations done in the 1960s and 1970s in Reykjavík, now the capital of Iceland, have unearthed possible traces of his homestead and fields.

Between 870 and 930, a flood of settlers arrived in Iceland, mostly from Norway. Good farmland was becoming increasingly scarce in Norway, and ambitious people were looking for open areas on which to raise crops and graze cattle. Also, the

King Fairhair of Norway greets a Danish chieftain.

tyrannical Harald Fairhair, king of Norway, was imposing strict rules on the people and stricter penalties for breaking them. Unwilling to lose their freedom and independence, a large number of nobles sold their lands, packed up their families, followers, slaves, livestock, and farming tools, and set sail for the new land.

By the year 930, the population of Iceland had reached about 30,000. Fierce and quarrelsome by nature, many of the settlers did not easily accept authority. Yet they believed in the rule of law. To maintain order, the settlers set up local assemblies called *Things* (from the Norwegian word for "assembly"). The Things made laws, settled

Axe River flows through Iceland's Thingvellir, where Viking chieftains met in a national assembly called the Althing.

disputes, and passed judgment on offenders. The membership included all the free adult men. They were led by the local chieftain, who was called the law-speaker.

In June 930, the 39 Things of Iceland sent their chieftains to meet in a national assembly, or Althing. Most scholars consider the Althing to be the world's first parliament or congress. The Althing met for about a week or two every summer in Iceland's Thingvellir ("Thing Fields"), a flat valley nestled between jagged cliffs about 30 miles northeast of Reykjavík. The representatives to the Althing voted by noisily rattling their weapons. In general, the louder the rattling, the higher the vote.

Sometime around the year 900, a Norwegian sailor named Gunnbjorn sighted—but did not land on—a rocky island about 200 miles west of Iceland. Decades later there lived in Iceland a hotheaded young man named Erik Thorvaldson. He was called Erik the Red because of the color of his hair. Around 980, Erik the Red accused a neighbor of failing to return some bench boards he had borrowed. When Erik went to reclaim his property by force, he got into a ferocious fight and killed several men, including two of the neighbor's sons.

Brought before the Thing at Thorsnes, Erik was banished from Iceland for three years. He decided to sail for the mysterious island that Gunnbjorn claimed to have seen.

At a meeting of the Althing, a father announces his daughter's divorce. Viking men and women could divorce their spouses at will.

For the next three years, Erik explored the rocky coasts of this unknown island. Then he returned to Iceland. Back home, Erik told of the new place, which he called Greenland, even though most of it was covered with ice and snow. As he said, "People would be the more eager to go there if it had a good name."

In 985, Erik collected a large group of settlers and led a fleet of 25 ships to Greenland. Only 14 ships completed the voyage. The rest sank or were driven back by bad weather.

Other ships followed over the next few years. Erik's followers established two settlements in Greenland: the Eastern Settlement and the Western Settlement. They built homes mainly along giant fjords, narrow ocean bays that are also found in Scandinavia. Here they farmed, fished, and raised cattle, hogs, and sheep. They also hunted bears and caribou, among other wild animals. Eventually there were about 3,000 settlers in Greenland. Erik ran a successful farm in Greenland until his death around the year 1000.

Over the following decades, the colonies on Greenland flourished. Ships went back and forth to Iceland and Norway, and there was much trade between these lands. Even so, life in Greenland was not easy.

The settlers tried to farm as they had in Scandinavia, but Greenland's harsher climate and shorter growing season led to frequent crop failures. The people had to depend on the sea for a full 80 percent of their diet. Attacks by Native Greenlanders made it even more difficult for the Viking settlers to maintain their colonies.

In the 1300s, the world temperature dropped, and sea ice started to block the passage of ships along the Greenland coast. Huge glaciers began to spread and cover the pastures and planting fields with ice. Eventually more and more Greenland settlers made their way back to Iceland or to Norway. The last recorded Viking event in Greenland was a church wedding held in 1408. By about 1450, the very last Vikings had packed up and left—or died.

Well before this happened, however, the Vikings had discovered another land. *The Greenlanders' Saga* tells what happened to a Viking sea captain, Bjarni Herjulfsson, and his crew when they were sailing from Iceland to Greenland around the year 986: "They put to sea as soon as they were ready and sailed for three days until land was lost to sight below the horizon. Then the fair wind failed and northerly gales and fog set in, and for many days they had no idea what their course was. After that, they saw the sun again and were able to get their bearings; they hoisted sail, and after a day's sailing they sighted land."

Experts now believe that the land Bjarni Herjulfsson and his crew spotted was the east coast of the North American continent. But Bjarni, whose goal was to make it to Greenland, steered

Viking settlers depended on the whale—depicted here as a big fish—for oil, bone, and meat.

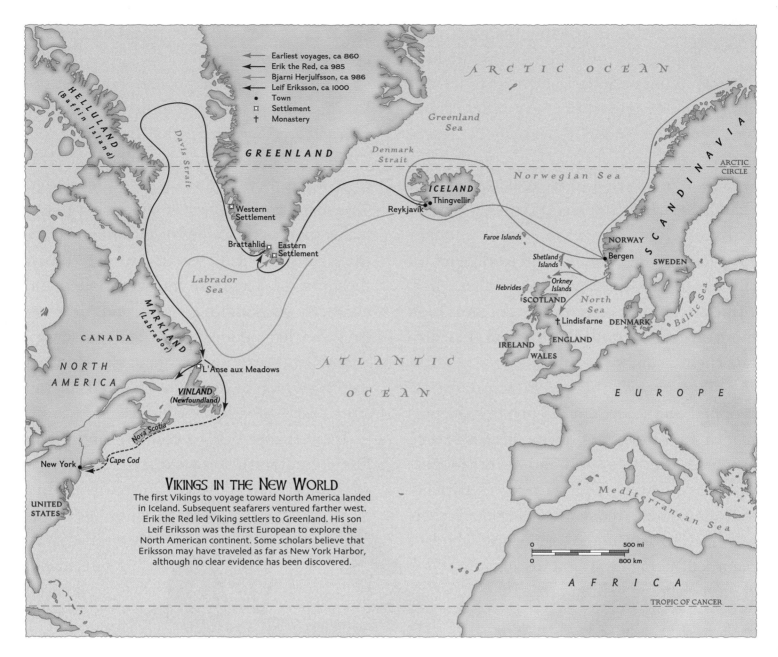

Legend:
← Earliest voyages, ca 860
← Erik the Red, ca 985
← Bjarni Herjulfsson, ca 986
← Leif Eriksson, ca 1000
• Town
⊡ Settlement
† Monastery

ARCTIC OCEAN

HELLULAND (Baffin Island)

Davis Strait

GREENLAND

Greenland Sea

Denmark Strait

Norwegian Sea

ARCTIC CIRCLE

ICELAND

⊡ Western Settlement

Reykjavik • Thingvellir

SCANDINAVIA

Brattahlid ⊡ ⊡ Eastern Settlement

Faroe Islands

NORWAY

Labrador Sea

Shetland Islands

Bergen

SWEDEN

Hebrides

Orkney Islands

MARKLAND (Labrador)

SCOTLAND

North Sea

Baltic Sea

CANADA

⊡ L'Anse aux Meadows

† Lindisfarne

DENMARK

NORTH AMERICA

VINLAND (Newfoundland)

IRELAND

ENGLAND

WALES

ATLANTIC OCEAN

EUROPE

Nova Scotia

New York • Cape Cod

UNITED STATES

Mediterranean Sea

VIKINGS IN THE NEW WORLD

The first Vikings to voyage toward North America landed in Iceland. Subsequent seafarers ventured farther west. Erik the Red led Viking settlers to Greenland. His son Leif Eriksson was the first European to explore the North American continent. Some scholars believe that Eriksson may have traveled as far as New York Harbor, although no clear evidence has been discovered.

0   500 mi
0   800 km

AFRICA

TROPIC OF CANCER

---

away from this unknown and mysterious land. Four days later, he arrived at his intended destination.

Bjarni told the settlers in Greenland of his discovery, but few of them showed any interest in exploring this new land. Only Erik the Red was attracted by the promising possibilities of a fresh discovery, and he organized an expedition to retrace Bjarni's voyage. On the way to the ship, however, Erik accidentally fell from his horse. Fearing the mishap signaled bad luck, he canceled the trip.

Around the year 1000, Leif Eriksson, the eldest son of Erik the Red, bought Bjarni's boat, gathered a group of 35 followers, and sailed west from Greenland to find the land that Bjarni had seen. Early sagas say that Eriksson came to a fertile land with a mild climate. This land was the east coast of either Canada or the United States, making Leif Eriksson the first known European to land on the North American continent.

Eriksson and his men came ashore in an area that he named Helluland ("Flat Rock Land"—perhaps modern Baffin Island). He then sailed farther south to a heavily wooded region that he called Markland ("Forestland"—perhaps Labrador). Continuing south, he went ashore at a place where he found grapes growing, which he called Vinland ("Wineland"). No one knows the exact location of Vinland because Eriksson left no maps.

In 1961, after seven years of excavation, archaeologists Helge Ingstad and Anne Stine Ingstad uncovered evidence of an old Viking settlement with perhaps 90 settlers in Newfoundland, Canada, at L'Anse aux Meadows. The Ingstads found the remains of eight longhouses with cooking pits similar to the Viking buildings in Iceland and Greenland and some

Heroic statue in Reykjavík, Iceland, idealizes Viking explorer Leif Eriksson, described by one saga as "a big, strapping fellow, handsome to look at, thoughtful and temperate in all things."

fire-cracked stones of a floor. Among their other discoveries were five sheds, where the settlers kept their boats during the winter. A few of the objects the Ingstads found that date back to Viking times include pins, a stone lamp, iron rivets, a needle sharpener, and several pieces of carved wood.

One building seemed to be a blacksmith's shop, with lumps of iron, a pile of slag, charcoal, a stone anvil, a hearth, a fire pit, and several scraps of iron and bronze that had been worked on. Laboratory tests showed that the charcoal and turf from the walls dated to around the year 1000, the time when Leif Eriksson set out west from Greenland.

Some scholars say that Eriksson's voyage ended in the region of Cape Cod, Massachusetts, or even farther south. Evidence for traveling as far as what is now New York City comes from Gunmar Eggertsson, a direct descendant of Leif Eriksson, who sailed from Iceland to New York in June 2000 in a reproduction of a Viking ship. Eggertsson quotes a passage in *Erik the Red's Saga* that describes Leif's trip down the east coast of North

Among the finds at L'Anse aux Meadows were items from a blacksmith's shop, depicted above.

America: "That spring the men sailed a long time, until they came to a river that flowed from the land into a lake and then into the sea. There were such large sandbars at its mouth that they could only get into the river at high tide."

According to Eggertsson and other experts, the only place that fits this description is New York City. The river is the Hudson and the lake is actually New York Harbor.

Many other scholars disagree. They point out that no traces of Viking activity have been found south of Newfoundland— except for one Viking coin unearthed in Maine.

The North American Viking colony at L'Anse aux Meadows lasted for only about three years. Nobody knows why the outpost was abandoned, but some historians theorize that the Vikings were driven out by native people, whom the colonists called Skraelings.

According to the sagas, Viking adventurers and explorers made several other voyages to the land called Vinland. But additional Skraeling attacks prevented settlers from

These reconstructions of sod-covered houses at L'Anse aux Meadows show how the settlement might have looked in Viking times.

establishing a permanent colony on the North American continent.

Vikings from Greenland probably continued to visit the continent for another 300 years or so. Traders brought lumber back, since trees were scarce in Greenland. They also brought back high-quality iron, which was used for making tools. To make up for the poor grain crops in Greenland, Viking merchants also collected grains for bread and beer on their trips. Such voyages ceased, however, as Greenland's Viking population dwindled.

CHAPTER SEVEN

THE VIKING SPIRIT

The Vikings, to be sure, wreaked much damage and mayhem on the lands and peoples they conquered. Yet most experts now believe that the Vikings were no more brutal or ruthless than other Europeans of the time. Furthermore, the Viking sense of personal freedom and many of the changes they brought about had a lasting impact on all of Western civilization.

Political and economic developments in Scandinavia during the Viking Age helped to create the strong and prosperous nations of Denmark, Norway, and Sweden, each under the rule of a single king. Viking invasions of England and France in the 800s and 900s led the people in these countries to stand together against the invaders. Under the Viking influence, unified countries developed where there had once been many small, divided kingdoms.

Viking warriors brought ideas of equality and democracy wherever they settled. The Icelandic Althing has often been regarded as the oldest parliament in the world. And although their society was divided into classes, the Vikings established the belief that all men were the same in the eyes of the law. When the Franks asked the Vikings who their leader was, they answered, "We have no lord, we are all equal." Even courtroom juries of 12 men and women come from an ancient Viking legal tradition.

Many of the great trade routes of the world were first established by the Vikings. As seafaring traders, the Vikings started and developed commerce in many corners of the world. Wherever they went, the Vikings built thriving new towns or enlarged old ones, such as Kiev in what is now Ukraine and Dublin in Ireland. A typical Viking trader might carry furs and slaves to Constantinople and Baghdad and return home with silks, spices, and precious metals.

Cast as one of the mythical maidens known as Valkyries, a singer performs in Richard Wagner's opera *The Valkyrie*. The 19-century composer based several operas on Viking legends. Costumes such as this perpetuate the mistaken idea that Vikings wore horned helmets.

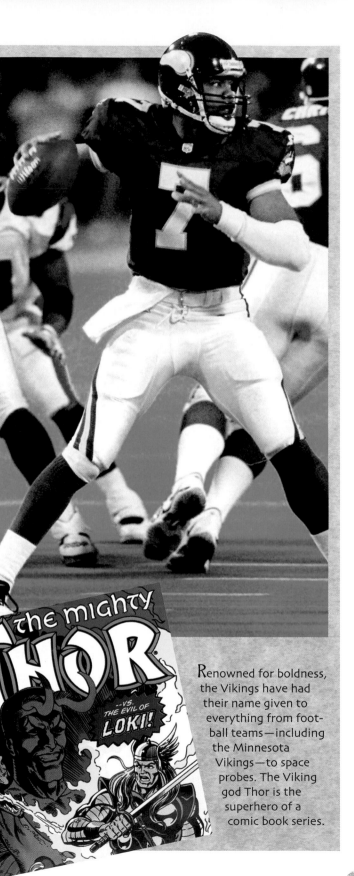

Renowned for boldness, the Vikings have had their name given to everything from football teams—including the Minnesota Vikings—to space probes. The Viking god Thor is the superhero of a comic book series.

The Vikings' shipbuilding skills enabled them to sail up the rivers of Europe and across the Atlantic Ocean. Their ship construction, the use of sails, and new methods of navigation contributed to their superb seamanship. Wherever they settled, they inspired local improvements in shipbuilding and sailing.

Viking skills and ideas for making weapons, tools, jewelry, coins, and objects for the home were widely copied. Ironmongers made excellent two-edged swords by twisting together several large iron bars and beating them flat. So strong were these swords that they did not shatter even when smashed with full force onto iron helmets or heavy metal shields.

The Vikings' switch from paganism to Christianity brought Scandinavia into the mainstream of predominantly Christian Europe. The Viking kings—Harald Bluetooth in Denmark, Hakon the Good in Norway, and Olaf Skotkonung in Sweden—were willing to be converted and to convert their people. This, combined with the zealous activity of Christian missionaries, made Christianity the sole religion of the Vikings by the end of the tenth century. Their overseas voyages helped spread the message of Christianity to places where it had not previously been introduced.

Elements of the Vikings' rich cultural heritage live on in many books, plays, poetry, and movies that they inspired. Some countries

Known as Jorvik in Viking times, the city of York in northern England takes pride in its Viking heritage , as illustrated by this sign outside a local hotel. Under the Vikings, who took over the city in 867, York became a prosperous trading and manufacturing center.

still celebrate a Midsummer holiday, which was a pagan Viking festival held in the middle of June. Many of our English words, such as "husband," "ugly," and "happy," come from Viking words. Even a football team, the Minnesota Vikings, has taken their name.

For the real Vikings, life was an endless struggle against cold, hunger, enemies, and the mysterious unknown. Men and women quickly learned to live and work in the face of many perils. All Vikings, warriors in particular, were taught to prize bravery, strength, and daring deeds. They knew that every battle, raid, or sea voyage might be the end of their life on earth. Viking myths taught that men who died bravely in battle could win fame and remembrance after death.

An unknown ninth-century Icelandic poet summed up the Vikings' highest goal in life this way:

"Cattle die,
    Kinsmen die,
    Each man dies himself.
    But fame
    Never dies,
    For anyone who wins a good name."

VIKING TIME CHART

Eleventh-century statuette of a Viking warrior, carved from elk horn.

793   Vikings from Norway raid England's Lindisfarne monastery. The event marks the start of the Viking Age.

841   Norwegian Vikings establish the town of Dublin, Ireland.

845   Danish Vikings attack Paris, France, for the first time.

859-862   Viking raiders sail down the French coast and into the Mediterranean Sea, attacking towns and cities along the way.

867   Danish Vikings capture York, England, and make it the base of their English kingdom.

870   Ingolf Arnason and a band of Vikings from Norway settle in Iceland.

886   Danish Vikings establish rule over half of England, an area named the Danelaw.

911   In exchange for protection against Viking invasion, the French give the Viking chieftain Rollo control of Normandy.

930   Icelanders establish the Althing.

985   Erik the Red leads settlers to Greenland and lays claim to the land.

ca 1000   Leif Eriksson explores the coast of North America.

1016   Canute of Demark consolidates Viking control over Norway, Denmark, and England.

1042   Edward the Confessor, an Englishman, is crowned king of England.

1066   William the Conqueror, from Normandy, successfully invades England and becomes king, bringing the Viking Age to a close.

ca 1200   Icelanders begin recording the sagas that had been passed down orally since the 800s.

54

INDEX

Resources

Further Reading

Ganeri, Anita. *Focus on Vikings*. New York: Franklin Watts, 1989.

Gravett, Christopher. *Going to War in Viking Times*. Danbury, Conn.: Franklin Watts, 2001.

Humble, Richard. *The Age of Leif Eriksson*. New York: Franklin Watts, 1989.

MacDonald, Fiona. *Vikings*. Hauppauge, N.Y.: Barron's, 1993.

Osborne, Mary Pope. *Favorite Norse Myths*. New York: Scholastic, 1996.

Sawyer, Peter, ed. *The Oxford Illustrated History of the Vikings*. New York: Oxford University Press, 1997.

Web Sites

Viking Age Club
www.vikingage.com
Covers many specific Viking topics.

Vikings: The North Atlantic Saga.
www.mnh.si.edu/vikings/
Details of the Smithsonian museum exhibit.

Medieval Scandinavia
www.medsca.org
Focus on medieval Scandinavia.

Authors' Bibliography

Fitzhugh, William, and Elizabeth I. Ward, eds. *Vikings: The North Atlantic Saga*. Washington, D.C.: Smithsonian Institution, 2000.

Gibson, Michael. *The Vikings*. Hove, England: Wayland, 1972.

Grant, Neil. *The Vikings*. New York: Oxford University Press, 1998.

Gravett, Christopher. *Going to War in Viking Times*. Danbury, Conn.: Franklin Watts, 2001.

Haywood, John. *Encyclopaedia of the Viking Age*. New York: Thames & Hudson, 2000.

MacDonald, Fiona. *Vikings*. Hauppauge, N.Y.: Barron's, 1993.

Magnusson, Magnus. *Vikings!* New York: Dutton, 1980.

Sawyer, Peter, ed. *The Oxford Illustrated History of the Vikings*. New York: Oxford University Press, 1997.

Simpson, Jacqueline. *The Viking World*. New York: St. Martin's Press, 1980

Vesilind, Priit J. "In Search of Vikings." *National Geographic,* May 2000, 2-27.

Wernick, Robert, and the editors of Time-Life Books. *The Vikings* (The Seafarers series). Alexandria, Va.: Time-Life Books, 1979.

When Longships Sailed: Vikings (What Life Was Like series). By the editors of Time-Life Books. Alexandria, Va.: Time-Life Books, 1998.

Sources for Quotations

The quotations in this book are taken from the following sources, which are cited above: Page 15: Gibson, 38; Page 17: MacDonald, 24; Page 21: Simpson, 151; Page 44: Magnusson, 214; Page 45: Gibson, 108; Page 47: Wernick, 149; Page 48: Gibson, 113; Page 51: Gibson, 119; Page 53: MacDonald, 48.

Design Notes

Since I was born in Iceland and my ancestors are from Iceland and the Faroe Islands, it was important to me that the design of this book reflect the culture from which it was born. The layout of this book was inspired by the designs of 17th-century manuscripts of Icelandic sagas. The display font used, Celtic Hand, is based on early Celtic (Irish) manuscripts, which were also inspired by Icelandic saga manuscripts. —BHJ